My Guardian Angel

Illustrated by
Samuel J. Butcher

The Regina Press
New York

Presented to

Andrea   Patten

From

Your Godmother
Aunt Linda

Date

March 26, 1995

Each fluffy cloud up in the sky
Has a special place
Where angels learn just how to fly
And share their gentle grace.

O nce upon a long ago
An angel learned to fly.
At first he flew a bit too low
But soon he touched the sky.

This angel and a butterfly
Upon a cloud did meet.
Together they soared through the sky
To watch a little one so sweet!

Each angel needs someone to love
To keep his halo bright,
Someone he'll watch from up above
And teach him wrong from right.

Angels study hard for years
To know just what to do
To stop a baby's flood of tears
And make her smile, too.

Did you hear the latest?
My baby's soft and sweet.
His smile is just the greatest.
He's such a special treat!

As gentle as a butterfly
A guardian angel came.
She sings the sweetest lullaby
And softly speaks her baby's name.

Silver are the angels' wings,
Golden is their hair,
They have a song of love to sing
And happiness to share.

A child's heart will flower
And bloom more every day,
As angels watch each hour
And guide them as they play.

A little angel shines above,
His light has golden wings.
His heart is filled with all the love
That every new life brings.

E ven as the sun does rise
And shine upon our day
We'll know we're watched with loving eyes
To guide us on our way.

Grammas' hugs and puppy love
Both get their joyful start
From an angel up above,
Who's aim is for the heart.

Little angel up above,
Her halo shines so bright.
She fills each child's heart with love
And keeps them warm at night.

An angel's waiting for the day
He has a life to share.
Happily he'll light their way
With special love and care.

As pure as a snowfall
Is the angels' work and play.
The joy they bring to one and all
Can warm us every day.

If ever we should need a lift
Our angels lend a hand.
It is their very special gift
To love and understand.

Each and every sadness
Our guardian angels feel,
But they also share our gladness
When our hearts begin to heal.

Happily the angels give
Us knowledge and impart
Wisdom by which we can live
And lessons of the heart.

This Angel's little rainbow
Reminds us of God's love.
Blue and pink and all the rest
Are gifts from up above.

Little angel up above
In the sky so blue,
Fill this child's heart with love
And guide him all day through.

$\mathbf{A}$ngels work so hard to be
Helpful, sweet, and true.
But sometimes, maybe, they could use
A little help from you.

_Safe within your angel's love
you're growing every day
She watches you from above
And helps you on your way.

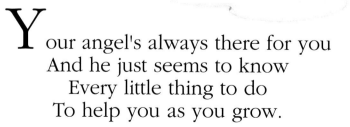

Your angel's always there for you
And he just seems to know
Every little thing to do
To help you as you grow.

From the fluffy clouds above
The angels' work is done.
They shower us with tender love
And warm us like the sun.

An angel's heart is very bright
With love to light your way.
Although you see it just at night
You feel his love each day.

Let peace and joy grow everyday
And love shine every night
And light our little angel's way
to keep us in his sight.

When a child needs a lift
God sends His angel there
And this is childhood's greatest gift,
To be safe in His care.

Slumbering in Heaven's grace
Brings dreams so sweet and pure.
No cares will cross this child's face,
Baby knows His love is sure.

Guardian Angel Prayer

Oh Angel of God
my Guardian dear
to whom God's love
commits me here.
Ever this day
be at my side
to light and guard
to rule and guide.
Amen.